D0405824

The Wasp in a Wig

LEWIS CARROLL

The Wasp in a Wig

A "Suppressed" Episode of

THROUGH THE LOOKING-GLASS AND WHAT ALICE FOUND THERE

With a Preface, Introduction and Notes by

MARTIN GARDNER

Clarkson N. Potter, Inc./Publishers NEW YORK
DISTRIBUTED BY CROWN PUBLISHERS, INC.

This book has been edited by Edward Guiliano. It was first printed for the Lewis Carroll Society of North America, Inc., and was issued in wrappers as well as in a deluxe format of 750 numbered copies.

FIRST AMERICAN TRADE EDITION

Library of Congress Catalog Card Number: 77-17089

ISBN: 0–517–532662

Manufactured in the United States of America

Second printing, April, 1978

Acknowledgements

THE PUBLICATIONS COMMITTEE of the Lewis Carroll Society of North America is proud to have arranged for this first American trade publication of a long-lost episode of *Through the Looking-Glass* with Clarkson Potter, Publishers, of New York City. Since its inception, the Society has enjoyed a close relationship with Potter, the leading publisher of Lewis Carroll material in America, and several members of our Publications Committee have had long and productive dealings with the Potter editorial staff.

On behalf of the Committee I would like to thank those who helped bring this project to fruition. Above all, we are indebted to Norman Armour, Jr., owner of the episode and Martin Gardner, a member of the Publications Committee.

Peter Heath, Morton N. Cohen, David H. Schaefer, and Stan Marx, also members of the Publications Committee, read and commented on this book during its various stages of production. The Publications Committee gratefully acknowledges Dorothy Rolph, Michael Hearn, John Shaw, Donald L. Hotson, J. A. Lindon, Alexander D. Wainwright, and Maxine Schaefer for their help.

We acknowledge the Trustees of the Dodgson Estate, Philip Jaques and Elisabeth Christie, for permission to print the episode and for their support of our publications program. We thank John Fleming of New York City and the Sotheby Parke Bernet staff in London for their cooperation.

Finally, we must thank Lewis Carroll for preserving this surprise un-birthday present for us.

—Edward Guiliano

Contents

Preface

IN 1974 the London auctioneering firm of Sotheby Parke Bernet and Company listed, inconspicuously, the following item in their June 3 catalog:

> Dodgson (C.L.) "Lewis Carroll." Galley proofs for a suppressed portion of "Through the Looking-Glass," slip 64-67 and portions of 63 and 68, with autograph revisions in black ink and note in the author's purple ink that the extensive passage is to be omitted.
>
> The present portion contains an incident in which Alice meets a bad-tempered wasp, incorporating a poem of five stanzas, beginning "When I was young, my ringlets waved." It was to have appeared following "A very few steps brought her to the edge of the brook" on page 183 of the first edition. The proofs were bought at the sale of the author's furniture, personal effects, and library, Oxford, 1898, and are apparently unrecorded and unpublished.

The word "apparently" in the last sentence was an understatement. Not only had the suppressed portion not been published, but Carroll experts did not even know it had been set in type, let alone preserved. The discovery that it still existed was an event of major significance to Carrollians—indeed, to all students of English literature. The book you now hold, more than one hundred years after *Through the Looking-Glass* was first set in type, is the first publication of the long-lost episode.

Until 1974 nothing was known about the missing portion beyond what Stuart Dodgson Collingwood, a nephew of Lewis Carroll, had said about it in his 1898 biography of his uncle, *The Life and Letters of Lewis Carroll.* Collingwood writes:

> The story, as originally written, contained thirteen chapters, but the published book consisted of twelve only. The omitted chapter introduced a wasp, in the character of a judge or barrister, I suppose, since Mr. Tenniel wrote that "a *wasp* in a *wig* is altogether beyond the appliances of art." Apart from difficulties of illustration, the "wasp" chapter was not considered to be up to the level of the rest of the book, and this was probably the principal reason of its being left out. (p. 146)

These remarks were followed by a facsimile of a letter, dated June 1, 1870, that John Tenniel had sent to Carroll. (The letter is here reproduced on pages xii–xiv.) In Tenniel's sketch for the railway carriage scene, Alice sits opposite a goat and a man dressed in white paper while the Guard observes Alice through opera glasses. In his final drawing Tenniel gave the man in the paper hat the face of Benjamin Disraeli, the British prime minister he so often caricatured in *Punch.*

Carroll accepted both of Tenniel's suggestions. The "old lady," presumably a character in the original version of Chapter 3, vanished from both the chapter and from Tenniel's illustration, and the Wasp vanished from the book. In *The Annotated Alice* my note on this ends: "Alas, nothing of the missing chapter has survived." Collingwood himself had not read the episode. We know this because he assumed, mistakenly as it turned out, that if the Wasp wore a wig he must have been a judge or lawyer.

Carroll left no record of his own final opinion of the episode or the poem it contained. He did, however, carefully preserve the galleys, and it seems likely that he intended to do something with them someday. It was Carroll himself, remember, who decided to publish his first version of *Alice in Wonderland,* the manuscript he had hand-lettered and illustrated for Alice Liddell. Many of his early poems, printed in obscure periodicals or not published at all, found their way eventually into his books. Even if Carroll had no specific plans for making use of the Wasp episode or its poem, it is hard to believe he would not have been pleased to know it would find eventual publication.

After Carroll's death in 1898 the galleys were bought by an unknown person and—for the present at least—we know little about who owned them until Sotheby's put them up for auction. They are not listed in the 1898 catalogs of Carroll's effects, apparently because they were included in a miscellaneous lot of unidentified items. "The property of a gentleman" is how Sotheby's labelled them in its catalog. Sotheby's does not disclose the identities of vendors who desire to remain anonymous, but they tell me that the galleys had been passed on to the vendor by an older member of his family.

The galleys were bought by John Fleming, a Manhattan rare book dealer, for Norman Armour, Jr., also of New York City. It is Mr. Armour's gracious consent to permit publication of these galleys that makes this book possible. What more need be said in the way of thanks?

4823

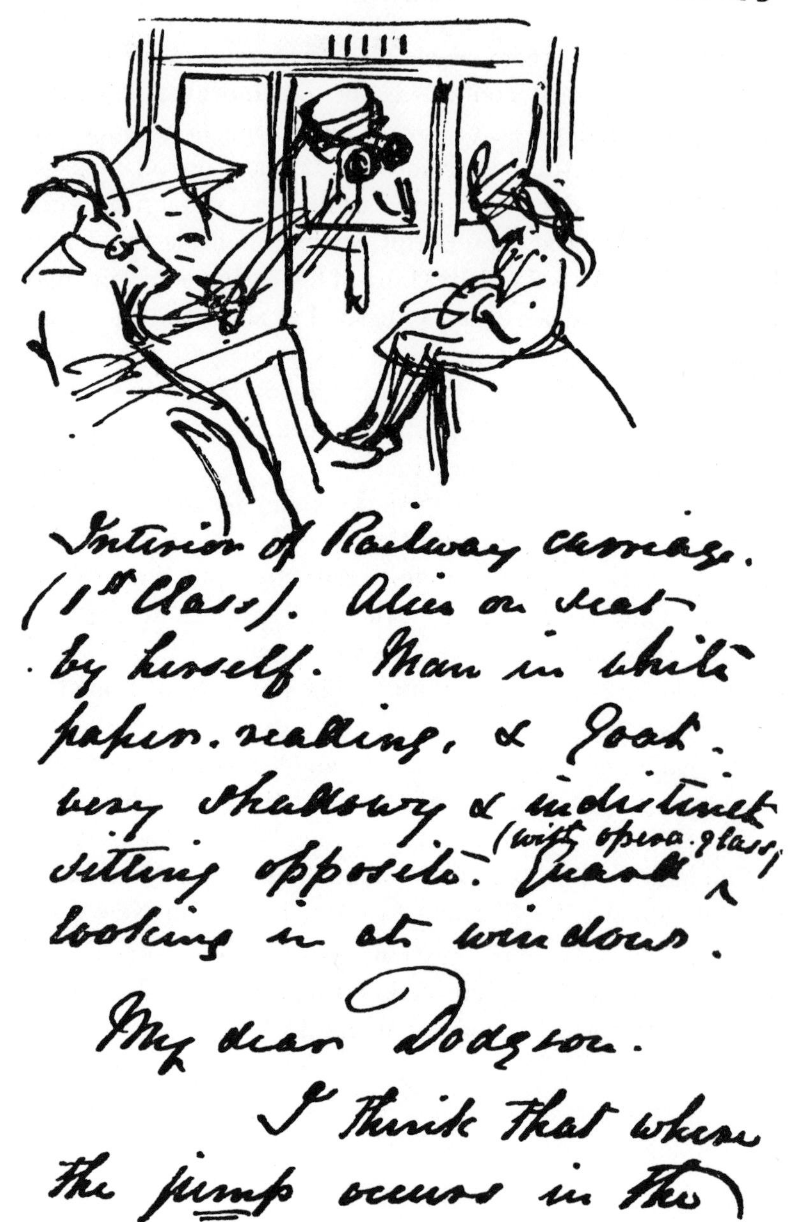
Interior of Railway carriage. (1st Class). Alice on seat by herself. Man in white paper. reading, & Goat. very shadowy & indistinct sitting opposite. Guard (with opera glass) looking in at window.

My dear Dodgson.

I think that where the jump occurs in the

Railway Scene you might
very well make Alice lay
hold of the Goat's beard
as being the object nearest
to her hand — instead of
the old lady's hair. The
jerk would naturally
throw them together.
Don't think me brutal, but
I am bound to say that
the 'wasp' chapter doesn't
interest me in the least, &
~~that~~ I can't see my way
to a picture. If you
want to shorten the book,

I can't help thinking —
with all submission —
that there is your oppor-
tunity.
In an agony of haste
Yours sincerely
J Tenniel.

Portsdown Road.
June 1. 1870

Figure 1. Facsimile of Tenniel's letter to Dodgson with a transcription.

My dear Dodgson.

I think that when the *jump* occurs in the Railway scene you might very well make Alice lay hold of the Goat's *beard* as being the object nearest to her hand —instead of the old lady's hair. The jerk would naturally throw them together.

Don't think me brutal, but I am bound to say that the '*wasp*' chapter doesn't interest me in the least, & I can't see my way to a picture. If you want to shorten the book, I can't help thinking—with all submission—that *there* is your opportunity.

In an agony of haste

Yours sincerely
J. Tenniel.

Portsdown Road.
June 1. 1870

The Wasp in a Wig

Introduction

BEFORE THE WASP episode came to light, most students of Carroll assumed that the lost episode was adjacent to, at least not far from, the railway carriage scene. This was because Tenniel, in his letter of complaint, seemed to link the two incidents. In Chapter 3, where Alice leaps the first brook and the train jumps over the second, Alice encounters a variety of insects, including bees the size of elephants. Was it not appropriate that she would meet a wasp in this region of the chessboard?

That Carroll did not intend Alice to come upon the Wasp so early in the chess game is evident at once from the numbers on the galleys, and from what Alice thought when the Wasp told her how his ringlets used to wave. "A curious idea came into Alice's head. Almost every one she had met had repeated poetry to her, and she thought she would try if the Wasp couldn't do it too." The first person to recite poetry to Alice is Tweedledee, and the second is Humpty Dumpty. The lost episode, therefore, had to occur later than Chapter 6.

The broken type on the first line of the galleys leave no doubt that Sotheby's catalog correctly indicates where Carroll had intended the Wasp episode to go. (The spot is shown by the arrow in Fig. 2, a reproduction of page 183 of the first edition of *Through the Looking-Glass,* here printed on page 12.) Alice has just waved her final farewell to the White Knight, then gone down the hill to leap the last brook and become a Queen. "A very few steps brought her to the edge of the brook." Instead of a period there was a comma. The sentence continued as at the top of the first galley: "And she was just going to spring over, when she heard a deep sigh, which seemed to come from the wood behind her."

An interesting question now arises that cannot be answered yet with certainty. Was the Wasp incident part of the White Knight chapter, or was it a separate chapter? If a separate chapter, then presumably there were short sections at the beginning and at the end of the galleys that were removed and used to splice together the present ending of Chapter 8. Perhaps the lost chapter began with Alice's words, "I hope it encouraged him," and ended with the three paragraphs that begin with her exclamation, "The Eighth square at last!"

Both Tenniel and Collingwood called the episode a "chapter," but there are difficulties with this view. The galleys give no indication that they are anything but an excerpt from Chapter 8, and it seems unlikely that Carroll would have wanted his second *Alice* book to have thirteen chapters when the first book had twelve. It is Morton Cohen's belief that Tenniel, writing "in an agony of haste," used the word "chapter" when he meant episode. Collingwood's remarks are easily explained as elaborations of how he interpreted Tenniel's letters. (There must have been at least one other Tenniel letter available to him because the remark of Tenniel's that he quotes, about a wasp in a wig being beyond the appliances of art, does not appear in the letter he reproduces in facsimile.)

One might argue that had the Wasp episode belonged to the White Knight chapter, the chapter would have been uncommonly long, and would not Tenniel have written that the episode should be removed to "shorten the chapter" rather than "shorten the book"? On the other hand, the fact that the chapter was too long may have been another reason why Carroll was willing to excise the episode. Unfortunately no other galleys for the book are known to have survived, so we are forced to rely on indirect evidence for deciding which view is correct.

Edward Guiliano favors the view that Tenniel had "episode" in mind. He supports the arguments already presented, and also feels that the incidents of the episode would have added thematic unity to the White Knight chapter. After conversing with the White Knight, an upperclass gentleman still in his vigor, Alice meets a lower-class worker in his declining years.* She waves goodbye to the White Knight with a handkerchief; the Wasp has a handkerchief around his face. The White Knight talks about bees and honey; the Wasp thinks Alice is a bee and asks her if she has any honey. Even the pun about the comb, Guiliano believes, is not quite so feeble in the context of the chapter as originally planned. These and other incidents in the Wasp episode link into the White Knight chapter in ways that suggest it was not intended to stand alone.

Was the Wasp episode worth preserving? It was, of course, eminently worth saving for historical reasons, but that is not what I mean. Does it have intrinsic merit?

---

* The White Knight, so far as Carroll's text alone is concerned, could have been a young man in his twenties. Tenniel, with Carroll's approval, drew him as an elderly gentleman, though certainly not as old as the "aged aged man" about whom the Knight sings.

Tenniel said it did not interest him in the least, and many who have recently read the episode agree that it is not (in Collingwood's words) "up to the level of the rest of the book." Peter Heath feels that one reason the episode lacks the vivacity of other parts of the book is that it repeats so many themes that occur elsewhere. Alice had a previous conversation with an unhappy insect (the Gnat) in Chapter 3. In the chapter following the Wasp episode Alice converses with another elderly, lower-class male, the Frog. The Wasp's criticisms of Alice's face are reminiscent of Humpty Dumpty's criticisms. Alice's attempts to repair the Wasp's disheveled appearance parallel her attempts to remedy the untidyness of the White Queen in Chapter 5. There are other echoes of familiar themes that Professor Heath has noted. "It's as if Carroll's inventiveness was flagging a bit," he writes in a letter, "and the momentum of the narrative had temporarily been lost."

All this may be true, but I am convinced that if the episode is read carefully, then reread several times on later occasions, its merit will steadily become more apparent. First of all it is unmistakably Carrollian in its general tone, its humor, its word play, and its nonsense. The Wasp's remark, "Let it stop there!" and his observation that Alice's eyes are so close together (compared to his own, of course) that she could have done as well with one eye instead of two, are both pure Carroll. The word play may not be up to Carroll's best, but we must remember that he frequently had a book set in type long before he began to work in earnest on revisions. If the Wasp episode was removed from the book before Carroll began to polish the galleys, it would explain why the writing seems cruder at times than elsewhere in the book.

Two features of the episode impress me as having special interest: the extraordinary skill with which Carroll, in just a few pages of dialog, brings out the personality of a waspish but somehow lovable old man, and Alice's unfailing gentleness toward him.

Although Alice is usually kind and respectful toward the curious creatures she meets in her two dreams, no matter how unpleasant the creatures are, this is not always the case. In the pool of tears she twice offends the Mouse by telling him that her cat chases mice and how a neighbor's dog likes to kill rats. A short time later, after the Caucus-race, she forgets herself again and insults the assembled birds by remarking on how much her cat likes to eat birds. And remember Alice's sharp kick that sends Bill, the Lizard, out the chimney? ("There goes Bill!")

In *Through the Looking-Glass,* Alice (now six months older) is not quite so thoughtless, but there is no episode in the book in which she treats a disagreeable creature with such remarkable patience. In no other episode, in either book, does her character come through so vividly as that of an intelligent, polite, considerate little girl. It is an episode in which extreme youth confronts extreme age. Although the Wasp is constantly critical of Alice, not once does she cease to sympathize with him.

Need I spell it out? We are told how much Alice, the white pawn, longs to become a Queen. We know how easily she could have leaped the final brook to occupy the last row of the chessboard. Yet Alice does not make the move when she hears the sigh of distress behind her. When the Wasp responds crossly to her kind remarks, she excuses his ill-temper with the understanding that it is his pain that makes him cross. After she has helped him around the tree to a warmer side, his response is "Can't you leave a body alone?" Unoffended, Alice offers to read to him from the wasp newspaper at his feet.

Although the Wasp continues to criticize, when Alice leaves him she is "quite pleased that she had gone back and given a few minutes to making the poor old creature comfortable." Carroll surely must have wanted to show Alice performing a final deed of charity that would justify her approaching coronation, a reward that Carroll, a pious Christian and patriotic Englishman, would have regarded as a crown of righteousness. Alice comes through as such an admirable, appealing little girl that Professor Guiliano discovered to his surprise that reading the episode altered a bit his response to the entire book.

The old man, with his waspish temper and his aching bones, is also, of course, a genuine insect. Female wasps (queens and workers) prey on other insects, such as caterpillars, spiders and flies, which they first paralyze by stinging. With their strong mandibles they remove the victim's head, legs and wings, then the body is chewed to a pulp to give as food to their larvae. It may not be accidental that Carroll's insect belongs to a social structure that includes fierce, powerful queens like the queens of chess and many former queens of England.

In contrast, male wasps (drones) have no stings. In some species the male, if you seize him in your hand, will try to frighten you into dropping him by going through all the movements of stinging. (John Burroughs likened this bluffing to a soldier in battle who tries to frighten the enemy by firing blank cartridges.) Male wasps, like Carroll's Wasp, although they look formidable, resemble the kings of chess. They are amiable, harmless creatures.

Except for a few hibernating queens, wasps are summer insects that do not survive the winter. During the hot months they work furiously to provide for their offspring, then they stiffen and die with the approach of autumn's cold winds. This is how Oliver Goldsmith phrases it in his marvelous, now forgotten *History of the Earth and Animated Nature:*

> While the summer heats continue, they [wasps] are bold, voracious, and enterprising; but as the sun withdraws, it seems to rob them of their courage and activity. In proportion as the cold increases, they are seen to become more domestic; they seldom leave the nest, they make but short adventures from home, they flutter about in the noon-day heats, and soon after return chilled and feeble. . . . As the cold increases they no longer find sufficient warmth in their nests, which grow hateful to them, and they fly to seek it in the corners of houses, and places that receive an artificial heat. But the winter is still insupportable; and, before the new year begins, they wither and die. . . ." (Vol. 4, Part 6, Bk. 4, Chap. 3, "The Wasp")

Like so many elderly people, the Wasp has happy memories of a childhood when his tresses waved. In five stanzas of doggerel he tells Alice about his terrible mistake of allowing friends to persuade him to shave his head for a wig. All his subsequent unhappiness is blamed on this foolish indiscretion. He knows his present appearance is ridiculous. His wig does not fit. He fails to keep it neat. He resents being laughed at. The Wasp is Oliver Wendell Holmes' "last leaf," enduring the community's ridicule as he clings "to the old forsaken bough."

Although the Wasp pretends not to want Alice to help

him in any way, his spirits are lifted by her visit and the opportunity to tell his sad tale. Indeed, before Alice leaves he has become animated and talkative. When she finally says good-bye he responds with "Thank ye." It is the only thanks Alice gets from anyone she meets on the mirror's other side.

The fashion of wearing wigs reached absurd heights in France and England in the seventeenth and eighteenth centuries. During Queen Anne's reign almost every upper-class man and woman in England wore a wig, and one could instantly tell a man's profession by the kind of wig he sported. Some male wigs hung below the shoulders to cover both back and chest. The craze began to fade under Queen Victoria. In Carroll's time it had all but vanished except for the ceremonial wigs of judges and barristers, the wigs of actors, and the wearing of wigs to conceal baldness. The Wasp's wig is clearly a mark of his advanced age even though he started wearing it when young.

Why a yellow wig? If the Wasp's ringlets were yellow it would be natural for him to substitute a yellow wig, but Carroll seems to emphasize the color for other reasons. He calls it "bright yellow." And when Alice first meets the Wasp his wig is covered by a yellow handkerchief tied around his head and face.

Both *Alice* books contain inside jokes about persons the real Alice, Alice Liddell, knew. It is possible, I suppose, that Carroll's Wasp pokes fun at someone, perhaps an elderly tradesman in the area, who sported an unkempt yellow wig that resembled seaweed.

Another theory has to do with the yellow color of many wasps in England. The American term "yellow-jackets," for a large class of social insects that were (and are) called hornets, may have been in Carroll's mind. The term had spread to England, and numerous varieties of British wasps have bright yellow stripes circling their black bodies. Wasp antennae are composed of tiny joints that also could be called ringlets. A young wasp's antennae would certainly wave, curl and crinkle as the poem has it. If cut off perhaps they would not grow again.

There may have been wasps in Oxford, familiar to Carroll and Alice Liddell, with black heads circled by a yellow stripe that would look for all the world like a yellow handkerchief tied around the insect's face. Even aside from a yellow stripe, a wasp's face does resemble a human face done up in a handkerchief, the knot's ends sticking up from the top of the head like two antennae. ** Professor Heath recalls having had just such thoughts himself when he was a child in England.

A third theory is that the Wasp, with his yellow handkerchief above a yellow wig, parallels Alice after she becomes a Queen—the gold crown on top of her flaxen hair.

A fourth theory (of course these theories are not mutually exclusive) is that Carroll chose yellow because of its long association in literature and common speech with autumn and old age. There is the yellow complexion of the elderly, especially if they suffer from jaundice. It is the color of fall leaves, of ripe corn, of paper "yellowed with age."

** Lewis Carroll's library at the time of his death included a book by John G. Wood called *A World of Little Wonders: or Insects at Home.* The chapter on wasps describes a common variety of social wasp as having antennae with a first joint that is "yellow in front."

"Sorrow, thought, and great distress," wrote Chaucer (in *Romance of a Rose*), "made her full yellow."

Shakespeare frequently used yellow as a symbol of age. Professor Cohen reports that Carroll, at least twice in his letters, quotes the following remark from *Macbeth*: "My way of life is fallen into the sere, the yellow leaf." These lines from Shakespeare's "Sonnet 73" are particularly apt:

> That time of year thou mayst in me behold
> When yellow leaves, or none, or few, do hang
> Upon those boughs which shake against the cold . . .

Through the Looking-Glass opens and closes with poems that speak of winter and death. The dream itself occurs in November while Alice sits in front of a blazing fire and snow is "kissing" the windowpanes. "Autumn frosts have slain July" is how Carroll puts it in his terminal poem, recalling that sunny July 4 boating trip on the Isis when he first told Alice the story of her trip to Wonderland.

Although Carroll was not yet forty when he wrote his second Alice book, he was twenty years older than Alice Liddell, the child-friend he adored above any other. In the book's prefatory poem he speaks of himself and Alice as "half a life asunder." He reminds Alice that it will not be long until the "bitter tidings" summon her to "unwelcome bed," and he likens himself to an older child fretting at the approach of the final bedtime.

Carroll scholars believe that Carroll intended his White Knight—that awkward, inventive gentleman with the mild blue eyes and kindly smile who treated Alice with such uncharacteristic courtesy for someone behind the mirror—to be a parody of himself. Is it possible that Carroll regarded his Wasp as a parody of himself forty years later? Professor Cohen has convinced me that it is not possible. Carroll prided himself on being a Victorian gentleman. Under no circumstances would he have associated himself with a lower-class drone. Nonetheless, it seems to me that Carroll could not have written this episode without being acutely aware of the fact that the chasm of age between Alice and the Wasp resembled the chasm that separated Alice Liddell from the middle-aged teller of the story.

I am persuaded that Carroll, perhaps not consciously, spoke through his Wasp like a ventriloquist talking through a dummy when he has the Wasp exclaim—in a way that seems strangely out of place in the dialog—"Worrity, worrity! There never was such a child!"

comes of having so many things hung round the horse——" So she went on talking to herself, as she watched the horse walking leisurely along the road, and the Knight tumbling off, first on one side and then on the other. After the fourth or fifth tumble he reached the turn, and then she waved her handkerchief to him, and waited till he was out of sight.

"I hope it encouraged him," she said, as she turned to run down the hill: "and now for the last brook, and to be a Queen! How grand it sounds!" A very few steps brought her to the edge of the brook. "The Eighth Square at last!" she cried as she bounded across,

* * * * * *

* * * * *

* * * * * *

and threw herself down to rest on a lawn as soft as moss, with little flower-beds dotted about it here and there. "Oh, how glad I am to get here! And what *is* this on my head?" she

Figure 2. Where Carroll intended the episode to appear. Reproduction of first edition.

The Wasp in a Wig

. . . and she was just going to spring over, when she heard a deep sigh, which seemed to come from the wood behind her.

"There's somebody *very* unhappy there," she thought, looking anxiously back to see what was the matter. Something like a very old man (only that his face was more like a wasp) was sitting on the ground, leaning against a tree, all huddled up together, and shivering as if he were very cold.

"I don't *think* I can be of any use to him," was Alice's first thought, as she turned to spring over the brook:—— "but I'll just ask him what's the matter," she added, checking herself on the very edge. "If I once jump over, everything will change, and then I can't help him." [1]

So she went back to the Wasp——rather unwillingly, for she was *very* anxious to be a Queen.

"Oh, my old bones, my old bones!" he was grumbling on as Alice came up to him.

"It's rheumatism, I should think," Alice said to herself, and she stooped over him, and said very kindly, "I hope you're not in much pain?"

The Wasp only shook his shoulders, and turned his head away. "Ah, deary me!" he said to himself.

---

1. The abrupt changes of scenery that take place whenever Alice leaps a brook are intended to resemble the changes that occur in a chess game whenever a move is made, as well as the sudden transitions that occur in dreams.

"Can I do anything for you?" Alice went on. "Aren't you rather cold here?"

"How you go on!" the Wasp said in a peevish tone. "Worrity, worrity! There never was such a child!" [2]

Alice felt rather offended at this answer, and was very nearly walking on and leaving him, but she thought to herself "Perhaps it's only pain that makes him so cross." So she tried once more.

"Won't you let me help you round to the other side? You'll be out of the cold wind there."

The Wasp took her arm, and let her help him round the tree, but when he got settled down again he only said, as before, "Worrity, worrity! Can't you leave a body alone?"

"Would you like me to read you a bit of this?" Alice went on, as she picked up a newspaper which had been lying at his feet. [3]

"You may read it if you've a mind to," the Wasp said, rather sulkily. "Nobody's hindering you, that *I* know of."

So Alice sat down by him, and spread out the paper on her knees, and began. "*Latest News. The Exploring Party have made another tour in the Pantry, and have found five new lumps of white sugar, large and in fine condition. In coming back——*"

"Any brown sugar?" the Wasp interrupted.

---

2. *Worrit:* a slang noun in Carroll's time for worry or mental distress. The *OED* quotes Mr. Bumble (in Dickens' *Oliver Twist*): "A porochial life, ma'am, is a life of worrit and vexation and hardihood." "Worrity," spoken later by the Wasp, was another form of the noun commonly used by British lower classes.

3. If any insect had a newspaper it would be the social wasp. Wasps are great paper makers. Their thin paper nests, usually in hollow trees, are made from a pulp which they produce by chewing leaves and wood fiber.

Alice hastily ran her eye down the paper and said "No. It says nothing about brown."

"No brown sugar!" [4] grumbled the Wasp. "A nice exploring party!"

"*In coming back,*" Alice went on reading, "*they found a lake of treacle. The banks of the lake were blue and white, and looked like china. While tasting the treacle, they had a sad accident: two of their party were engulphed——*"

"Were *what*?" the Wasp asked in a very cross voice.

"En-gulph-ed," Alice repeated, dividing the word into syllables. [5]

"There's no such word in the language!" said the Wasp.

"It's in this newspaper, though," Alice said a little timidly.

"Let it stop there!" said the Wasp, fretfully turning away his head.

Alice put down the newspaper. "I'm afraid you're not

---

4. *Brown sugar:* Wasps are fond of all kinds of man-made sweets, especially sugar. Morton Cohen points out that the Wasp's preference for brown sugar is characteristic of Victorian lower classes who found it cheaper then than the refined white.

5. *Engulph:* a common spelling of "engulf" in the sixteenth and seventeenth centuries. It was occasionally seen in Carroll's time, and the Wasp may be voicing Carroll's personal dislike of the spelling. Perhaps it is Alice's incorrect pronunciation, "en-gulph-ed" (three syllables instead of two) that the Wasp finds so outlandish. Donald L. Hotson suggests that Carroll may here be playing on a university slang expression of the time. According to *The Slang Dictionary* (Chatto and Windus, 1974), "gulfed" (sometimes spelled "gulphed") was "originally a Cambridge term, denoting that a man is unable to enter for the classical examination from having failed in the mathematical. . . . The expression is common now in Oxford as descriptive of a man who goes in for honours, and only gets a pass."

well," she said in a soothing tone. "Can't I do anything for you?"

"It's all along of the wig," [6] the Wasp said in a much gentler voice.

"Along of the wig?" Alice repeated, quite pleased to find that he was recovering his temper.

"You'd be cross too, if you'd a wig like mine," the Wasp went on. "They jokes at one. And they worrits one. [7] And then I gets cross. And I gets cold. And I gets under a tree. And I gets a yellow handkerchief. [8] And I ties up my face— —as at the present."

Alice looked pityingly at him. "Tying up the face is very good for the toothache," she said. [9]

"And it's very good for the conceit," added the Wasp.

Alice didn't catch the word exactly. "Is that a kind of toothache?" she asked.

The Wasp considered a little. "Well, no," he said: "it's when you hold up your head——*so*——without bending your neck."

---

6. *All along of:* all because of. Another lower-class expression of the day.

7. *Worrit:* The word was also vulgarly used as a verb. "Don't worrit your poor mother," says Mrs. Saunders in Dickens' *Pickwick Papers.* The Wasp's speech marks him clearly as a drone in the wasp social structure.

Carroll not only identified his cantankerous, aged man with a creature universally feared and hated, he also made him lower class, in sharp contrast to Alice's upper-class background—facts that make her kindness toward the insect all the more remarkable.

8. A yellow silk handkerchief, colloquially called a "yellowman," was fashionable in Victorian England.

9. Tying a handkerchief around the face, with a poultice inside, was in Carroll's time believed around the world to provide relief from a toothache. Persons who considered themselves good looking must have frequently been seen in this condition, and their appearance surely would not have strengthened their conceit.

"Oh, you mean stiff-neck," [10] said Alice.

The Wasp said "That's a new-fangled name. They called it conceit in my time."

"Conceit isn't a disease at all," Alice remarked.

"It is, though," said the Wasp: "wait till you have it, and then you'll know. And when you catches it, just try tying a yellow handkerchief round your face. It'll cure you in no time!"

He untied the handkerchief as he spoke, and Alice looked at his wig in great surprise. It was bright yellow like the handkerchief, [11] and all tangled and tumbled about like a heap of sea-weed. "You could make your wig much neater," she said, "if only you had a comb."

"What, you're a Bee, are you?" the Wasp said, looking at her with more interest. "And you've got a comb. [12] Much honey?"

---

10. *Stiff-necked:* the episode's first pun. A stiff neck is a bodily ailment as well as the bearing of a haughty, proud or conceited person. Perhaps the Wasp is warning Alice of the danger of becoming a haughty Queen, as stiff-necked as an ivory chess queen. Indeed, as soon as Alice finds the gold crown on her head she walks about "rather stiffly" to keep the crown from falling off. In the last chapter she commands the black kitten to "sit up a little more stiffly" like the Red Queen she fancied the kitten to have been in her dream. Compare also with the "proud and stiff" messenger in Humpty Dumpty's poem.

Professor Cohen observes that the Wasp reverses history when he calls "stiff-neck" a new-fangled name. It is a much older word than "conceit." "You are a stiffnecked people," the Lord commanded Moses to tell the Israelites (Exodus 33:5).

11. *Bright yellow:* The phrase is used again by Carroll in Chapter 9 where it is also associated with advanced age. A "very old frog" is dressed in "bright yellow."

12. *Comb:* the episode's second pun. Note that if Alice is a bee, she is about to become a Queen bee.

"It isn't that kind," Alice hastily explained. "It's to comb hair with——your wig's so *very* rough, you know."

"I'll tell you how I came to wear it," the Wasp said. "When I was young, you know, my ringlets used to wave ——"

A curious idea came into Alice's head. Almost every one she had met had repeated poetry to her, and she thought she would try if the Wasp couldn't do it too. "Would you mind saying it in rhyme?" she asked very politely.

"It aint what I'm used to," said the Wasp: "however I'll try; wait a bit." He was silent for a few moments, and then began again—

"When I was young, my ringlets waved [13]
And curled and crinkled on my head:
And then they said 'You should be shaved,
And wear a yellow wig instead.'

---

13. Is this poem, like so many of the others in both *Alice* books, a parody? Many poems and songs of the time begin "When I was young, . . ." but I could find none that seemed a reasonable candidate for parody. Carroll may have been aware that the phrase "ringlets waved" occurs in John Milton's beautiful description of the naked Eve (*Paradise Lost*, Book 4):

She, as a veil down to the slender waist,
Her unadorned golden tresses wore
Dishevelled, but in wanton ringlets waved
As the vine curls her tendrils . . .

And there is the following line from Alexander Pope's "Sappho":

No more my locks, in ringlets, curled . . .

However, since ringlets always curl and wave, the parallels may be coincidental.

It may be worth pointing out that ringlets are not the naturally-curled hair of short locks, but long locks in helical form like the vines mentioned by Milton. As a mathematician Carroll knew that the helix is an asymmetrical structure which (in Alice's words) "goes the other way" in the mirror.

It is no accident that the second *Alice* book is filled with references to mirror reversals and asymmetric objects. The helix itself is mentioned several times. Humpty Dumpty compares the toves to corkscrews, and Tenniel drew them

But when I followed their advice,
And they had noticed the effect,
They said I did not look so nice
As they had ventured to expect.

They said it did not fit, and so
It made me look extremely plain:
But what was I to do, you know?
My ringlets would not grow again.

So now that I am old and gray,
And all my hair is nearly gone,
They take my wig from me and say
'How can you put such rubbish on?'

And still, whenever I appear,
They hoot at me and call me 'Pig!' [14]
And that is why they do it, dear,
Because I wear a yellow wig."

---

with helical tails and snouts. Humpty also speaks in a poem about waking up fish with a corkscrew, and in Chapter 9 the White Queen recalls how Humpty had a corkscrew in hand when he was looking for a hippopotamus. In Tenniel's pictures the unicorn and the goat have helical horns. The road that leads up the hill in Chapter 3 twists like a corkscrew. Carroll must have realized that the young (perhaps then conceited?) Wasp, admiring himself in a mirror, would have seen his ringlets curl the other way.

Any way you look at it, the poem itself is a strange one to appear in a book for children, though no more so, perhaps, than the inscrutable poem recited by Humpty in Chapter 6. The cutting off of hair, like decapitation and teeth extraction, is a familiar Freudian symbol of castration. Interesting interpretations of the poem will surely be forthcoming from psychoanalytically oriented critics.

14. In the Pig and Pepper chapter of *Alice in Wonderland,* Alice at first thinks that "Pig!", shouted by the Duchess, is addressed to her. It turns out that the Duchess is hurling it at the baby boy she is nursing, and who soon turns into an actual pig. The use of "pig" as a derisive name for a person,

"I'm very sorry for you," Alice said heartily: "and I think if your wig fitted a little better, they wouldn't tease you quite so much."

"*Your* wig fits very well," the Wasp murmured, looking at her with an expression of admiration: "it's the shape of your head as does it. Your jaws aint well shaped, though——I should think you couldn't bite well?"

Alice began with a little scream of laughter, which she turned into a cough as well as she could.[15] At last she managed to say gravely, "I can bite anything I want."[16]

"Not with a mouth as small as that," the Wasp persisted. "If you was a-fighting, now——could you get hold of the other one by the back of the neck?"

"I'm afraid not," said Alice.

---

says the *OED*, was common in Victorian England. Surprisingly, even then it was an epithet often used against police officers. An 1874 slang dictionary adds: "The word is almost exclusively applied by London thieves to a plain-clothes man."

J. A. Lindon, a British writer of comic verse, suggests that it is the Wasp's baldness (cf., the baldness of the Duchess' baby) that prompts the epithet; and he recalls the association of pig and wig in "piggywiggy," which the *OED* says is applied both to a little pig and a child. In "The Owl and the Pussy-cat," Edward Lear writes:

> And there in a wood a Piggy-wig stood,
> With a ring at the end of its nose.

15. Alice changed her "little scream of laughter" at the Wasp to a discreet cough. A short time before she had tried unsuccessfully to hold back a "little scream of laughter" at the White Knight. We cannot be sure, of course, that all parallels such as this were in the original text. After removing the Wasp episode Carroll may have borrowed some of its phrases and images for use elsewhere when he polished the rest of the galleys.

16. Alice once frightened her nurse by shouting in her ear, "So let's pretend that I'm a hungry hyaena and you're a bone!" (*Through the Looking-Glass*, Chapter 1.)

"Well, that's because your jaws are too short," the Wasp went on: "but the top of your head is nice and round." He took off his own wig as he spoke, and stretched out one claw towards Alice, [17] as if he wished to do the same for her, but she kept out of reach, and would not take the hint. So he went on with his criticisms.

"Then your eyes——they're too much in front, no doubt. One would have done as well as two, if you *must* have them so close——" [18]

Alice did not like having so many personal remarks made on her, and as the Wasp had quite recovered his spirits, and was getting very talkative, she thought she might safely leave him. "I think I must be going on now," she said. "Good-bye."

"Good-bye, and thank-ye," said the Wasp, and Alice tripped down the hill again, quite pleased that she had gone back and given a few minutes to making the poor old creature comfortable.

---

17. This somewhat terrifying scene, a large wasp reaching out a "claw" to remove Alice's hair, recalls three other episodes in the book. The White Knight, mounting his horse, steadies himself by holding Alice's hair. The White Queen grabs Alice's hair with both hands in Chapter 9. And, in a reversal of ages, when the railway carriage jumps the second brook we know, from Tenniel's letter, that Carroll planned to have Alice seize the hair of an old lady sitting nearby.

18. Unlike Alice, wasps have bulbous compound eyes on the sides of their heads, and large strong jaws. Like Alice their heads are "nice and round." Other looking-glass creatures (the Rose, the Tiger-lily, the Unicorn) size up Alice in similar fashion, in the light of their own physical attributes.

Tenniel, at the age of twenty, lost the sight of one eye in a fencing bout with his father. The button accidentally dropped from his father's foil, and the blade's tip flicked across his right eye with a sudden pain that must have felt like a wasp's sting. One can understand why Tenniel may have been offended by the Wasp's remark; if so, it could have colored his attitude toward the episode.

The Wasp in a Wig

Figure 3. Facsimile of corrected galley proofs of suppressed portion of Through the Looking-Glass. *(Slips 64-67 and portions of 63 and 68.) Carroll's revisions are in black ink. On slip 63 the order to "omit to middle of Slip 68," the cross striking out the section's opening, and the curved line on the left are in the author's purple ink as are the line on the left and order to "Omit" on Slip 68.*

and she was just going to spring over, when she heard a deep sigh, which seemed to come from the wood behind her.

"There's somebody *very* unhappy there," she thought, ~~and she went a little way~~ looking anxiously back ~~again~~ to see what was the matter. Something like a very old man (only that his face was more like a wasp) was sitting on the ground, leaning against a tree, all huddled up together, and shivering as if he were very cold.

Omit to middle of Slip 68 –

"I don't *think* I can be of any use to him," was Alice's first thought, as she turned to spring over the brook:——"but I'll just ask him what's the matter," she added, checking herself on the very edge. "If I once jump over, everything will change, and then I can't help him."

So she went back to the Wasp——rather unwillingly, for she was *very* anxious to be a Queen.

"Oh, my old bones, my old bones!" he was grumbling on, as Alice came up to him.

"It's rheumatism, I should think," Alice said to herself, and she stooped over him, and said very kindly "I hope you're not in much pain?"

The Wasp only shook his shoulders, and turned his head away. "Ah, deary me!" he said to himself.

"Can I do anything for you?" Alice went on. "Aren't you rather cold here?"

"How you go on!" the Wasp said in a peevish tone. "Worrity, worrity! There never was such a child!"

Alice felt rather offended at this answer, and was very nearly walking on and leaving him, but she thought to herself "Perhaps it's only pain that makes him so cross." So she tried once more.

"Won't you let me help you round to the

other side? You'll be out of the cold wind there."

The Wasp took her arm, and let her help him round the tree, but when he got settled down again he only said, as before, "Worrity, worrity! Can't you leave a body alone?"

"Would you like me to read you a bit of this?" Alice went on, as she picked up a newspaper which had been lying at his feet.

"You may read it if you've a mind to," the Wasp said, rather sulkily. "Nobody's hindering you, that *I* know of."

So Alice sat down by him, and spread out the paper on her knees, and began. "*Latest News. The Exploring Party have made another tour in the Pantry, and have found five new lumps of white sugar, large and in fine condition. In coming back——*"

"Any brown sugar?" the Wasp interrupted.

Alice hastily ran her eye down the paper and said "No; it says nothing about brown."

"No brown sugar!" grumbled the Wasp. "A nice exploring party!"

"*In coming back,*" Alice went on reading, "*they found a lake of treacle. The banks of the lake were blue and white, and looked like china. While tasting the treacle, they had a sad accident: two of their party were engulphed——* "

"Were *what?*" the Wasp asked in a very cross voice.

"En-gulph-ed," Alice repeated, dividing the word into syllables.

"There's no such word in the language!" said the Wasp.

"It's in this newspaper though," Alice said a little timidly.

"Let it stop there!" said the Wasp, fretfully turning away his head.

Alice put down the newspaper. "I'm afraid you're not well," she said in a soothing tone. "Can't I do anything for you?"

"It's all along of the wig," the Wasp said in a much gentler voice.

"Along of the wig?" Alice repeated, quite pleased to find that he was recovering his temper.

"You'd be cross too, if you'd a wig like

mine," the Wasp went on. "They jokes at one. And they worrits one. And then I gets cross. And I gets cold. And I gets under a tree. And I gets a yellow handkerchief. And I ties up my face——as at the present."

Alice looked pityingly at him. "Tying up the face is very good for the toothache," she said.

"And it's very good for the conceit," added the Wasp.

Alice didn't catch the word exactly. "Is that a kind of toothache?" she asked.

The Wasp considered a little. "Well, no," he said: "it's when you hold up your head——*so*——without bending your neck."

"Oh, you mean stiff-neck," said Alice.

The Wasp said "That's a new-fangled name. They called it conceit in my time."

"Conceit isn't a disease at all," Alice remarked.

"It is though," said the Wasp: "wait till you have it, and then you'll know. And when you catches it, just try tying a yellow handkerchief round your face. It'll cure you in no time!"

He untied the handkerchief as he spoke, and Alice looked at his wig in great surprise. It was bright yellow like the handkerchief, and all tangled and tumbled about like a heap of sea-weed. "You could make your wig much neater," she said, "if only you had a comb."

"What, you're a Bee, are you?" the Wasp said, looking at her with more interest. "And you've got a comb. Much honey?"

"It isn't that kind," Alice hastily explained. "It's to comb hair with——your wig's so *very* rough, you know."

"I'll tell you how I came to wear it," the Wasp said. "When I was young, you know, my ringlets used to wave——"

A curious idea came into Alice's head. Almost every one she had met had repeated poetry to her, and she thought she would try if the Wasp couldn't do it too. "Would you mind saying it in rhyme?" she asked very politely.

"It aint what I'm used to," said the Wasp: "however I'll try; wait a bit." He was silent for a few moments, and then began again—

"When I was young, my ringlets waved
And curled and crinkled on my head:
And then they said 'You should be shaved,
And wear a yellow wig instead.'

"But when I followed their advice,
And they had noticed the effect,
They said I did not look so nice
As they had ventured to expect.

"They said it did not fit, and so
It made me look extremely plain:
But what was I to do, you know?
My ringlets would not grow again.

"So now that I am old and gray,
And all my hair is nearly gone,
They take my wig from me and say
'How can you put such rubbish on?'

"*And still, whenever I appear,*
They hoot at me and call me 'Pig!'
And that is why they do it, dear,
Because I wear a yellow wig."

"I'm very sorry for you," Alice said heartily: "and I think if your wig fitted a little better, they wouldn't tease you quite so much."

"*Your* wig fits very well," the Wasp murmured, looking at her with an expression of admiration: "it's the shape of your head as does it. Your jaws aint well shaped, though—— I should think you couldn't bite well?"

Alice began with a little scream of laughing, which she turned into a cough as well as she could: at last she managed to say gravely "I can bite anything I want."

"Not with a mouth as small as that," the Wasp persisted. "If you was a-fighting, now ——could you get hold of the other one by the back of the neck?"

"I'm afraid not," said Alice.

"Well, that's because your jaws are too short," the Wasp went on: "but the top of your head is nice and round." He took off his own wig as he spoke, and stretched out one claw towards Alice, as if he wished to do the same for her, but she kept out of reach, and would not take the hint. So he went on with his criticisms.

Omit

"Then your eyes——they're too much in front, no doubt. One would have done as well as two, if you *must* have them so close——"

Alice did not like having so many personal remarks made on her, and as the Wasp had quite recovered his spirits, and was getting very talkative, she thought she might safely leave him. "I think I must be going on now," she said. "Good-bye."

"Good-bye, and thank-ye," said the Wasp, and Alice tripped down the hill again, quite pleased that she had gone back and given a few minutes to making the poor old creature comfortable.

THE WASP IN A WIG
has been designed by Dennis J. Grastorf
and printed by The Book Press, Brattleboro, Vermont,
on Bradford Offset. The text type is 11pt.
Modern No. 8 with Caslon Italic
for the display.

A Note about the Lewis Carroll Society

THE LEWIS CARROLL SOCIETY of North America is a nonprofit organization that encourages the study of the life, work, times, and influence of Charles Lutwidge Dodgson. The Society was founded in 1974 and has grown from several dozen members to several hundred members, drawn from across North America and from abroad. Current members include leading authorities on Carroll, collectors, students, general enthusiasts, and libraries. The Society is making a concerted, professional effort to become the center for Carroll activities and studies.

The Society meets twice a year, usually in the fall and in the spring, at the site of an important Carroll collection in the eastern United States. Meetings have featured distinguished speakers and outstanding exhibitions.

The Society maintains an active publications program, administered by a distinguished committee interested in publishing and assisting in the publication of materials dealing with the life and work of Lewis Carroll. Members receive the Society's newsletter, the *Knight-Letter,* three chapbooks in the Society's series, *Carroll Studies,* and other special publications. *The Wasp in a Wig* was first published as part of this series.

Further information can be obtained by writing to The Secretary, Lewis Carroll Society of North America, 617 Rockford Road, Silver Spring, Maryland 20902.